Beg Arc

REVISED EDITION

Roy K. Niemeyer
Michigan State University

Wadsworth Publishing Company, Inc.
Belmont, California

Third printing: December 1969

L.C. Cat. Card No.: 67-16022

Printed in the United States of America

CONTENTS

VALUES

The twang of a bowstring, the sight of an arrow speeding toward the gold, and the thud of an arrow hitting the target are thrills to a vast number of archers. By the millions they remain fascinated by the equipment that once served man as his chief weapon and means of survival. For modern man to have to depend on the bow and arrow for survival is almost unthinkable. Today, however, archery has found its place as a prominent sport in the life of modern man. What is it about this sport that keeps people participating and constantly attracts large numbers of newly interested people of all ages and both sexes?

It is difficult to point out any single reason for the popularity of archery. One of the physiological values derived is the development of strength and endurance, especially in the musculature of the shoulder girdle. The contracting of the abdominal and back muscles with the stretching of the chest muscles aid in the development and maintenance of proper posture. Valuable eye exercise is obtained through the intense concentration on a focal point during aiming. A substantial amount of all-round exercise is accrued through the walking and bending involved. It is for these reasons, and the fact that the sport is usually played in the healthful outdoors, that archery is a stimulating, invigorating pastime.

Social benefits for the archer include excellent opportunities to meet people of both sexes and all ages, to engage leisurely in the sport with a few friends on an informal basis, to compete extensively against others, to cooperate with other club members toward a common goal, to engage as a family in a recreational pursuit, or to understand human nature better through the opportunities provided while hunting and camping together.

There are other values in archery that are of a psychological nature. Real personal satisfaction can be derived through handling a bow competently. Fun, relaxation, and the sense of achievement that comes when you can place the arrow exactly where it is aimed are psychological benefits that help build self-confidence. The opportunity to get away from it all, to draw the bow and arrows and watch the arrows penetrate the target, may be just the thing to relieve pent-up emotions after a busy day. Another important psychological value is the pride of the bow hunter who bags his deer with a running shot at thirty yards or who finally gets his deer, maybe after ten fruitless years.

Perhaps the finest long-range benefit of archery is the length of time that one is able to enjoy it. Shooting merely for recreation, engaging in tournaments from the local to the national or international level, having an activity that the whole family can enjoy together, and hunting and fishing with the bow are among the many activities archers enjoy. Hunting and fishing often become the ultimate in archery for many people, and whatever else is done in shooting is done as preparation for them.

Archery is classified as an individual activity, because no other person need be present for complete participation. Activities of this nature are necessary in the repertory of those who claim to be physically educated. One cannot participate in vigorous team activities for a lifetime. Sports such as football and basketball usually prove to be too strenuous and undesirable for most people after the age of thirty or thirty-five. It therefore behooves the athlete to learn some individual recreational activities. Athletes who reach the age of forty-five tend to become less active than nonathletes and consequently gain more harmful weight. Perhaps this is because the athletes can no longer engage in vigorous sports and have not learned worthwhile leisure-time sports. On the other hand, the nonathletes who take time while they are young to learn carry-over sports participate more, become proficient, and eventually control their weight better.

It is well known that people will play the games they play well. Consequently, it behooves one to learn some individual activities at the earliest age possible and to learn them well. "Be active for life" is sound advice from a health standpoint.

Among the most obvious advantages of archery over many other activities offered in the physical education program are that it can be enjoyed the year around, outdoors and indoors; it is reasonably inexpensive; and it can be enjoyed for life. Another distinct advantage is that a lifelong hobby may be pursued in making archery equipment or collecting lore associated with archery.

HISTORY

The time and place of the origin of archery are not known, but drawings left by cavemen on the rock walls of their dwellings on the Spanish peninsula indicate that the bow and arrow were used at that time. Archaeologists estimate that archery was known about 100,000 years ago. It can safely be stated that the discovery of the bow and arrow was one of the most important cultural advances in the history of the human race. This discovery was certainly as important as the discovery of fire or the wheel, or the development of speech. Only after the bow was developed did man become superior to the wild animals of his day, and this superiority may have had a great influence on the very continuation of the human race.

THE DISCOVERY OF THE BOW

How archery was discovered can only be conjectured. Possibly a man idly experimenting with a tree branch that had a piece of vine, gut, or rawhide attached to it discovered that it could cast a light stick of wood farther than he could throw a heavier spear. As the idea developed, better pieces of wood were found for bows, and feathers or leaves were added to the sticks to guide them better in flight. The idea of adding sharp stones to the ends of the arrows was probably the next stage of development. Once the bow was perfected, it became man's most important weapon. We can imagine his feeling of relief when he no longer had to flee the beasts or to fight in close combat with clubs or spears or when he could take game at greater distances than previously.

THE WIDE USE OF THE BOW

The bow is thought to have been known to all Eastern Hemisphere tribes except the aboriginal Australians. The Israelites, Babylonians, Mongolians, Assyrians, Chinese, and Japanese all favored the bow and arrow. The Egyptians used bows and arrows in overthrowing the Persians and then successfully waged war on many other countries. The success of the bow and arrow as a weapon of war spread rapidly, and many nations gave up their chief weapons—slings and javelins—for this more efficient device.

The Greeks and Turks are credited with originating composite bows made of wood, horn, and sinew and shaped like a "C" when unstrung. These composite bows were extremely efficient. Interestingly, many of our modern bows tend to resemble them. An ancient Turkish bow is said to have shot an arrow more than 800 yards. This record flight was unsurpassed until Danny LaMore won the National Flight Championship at Lancaster, Pennsylvania, on August 17, 1959, with a free-style flight (bow held by the feet and pulled with both hands) of 937.17 yards and a regular flight (hand-held) of 850.67 yards. At the same meet Norma Beaver set a women's national record of 578.7 yards.

The bow was the chief weapon of warfare for centuries—until the battle of the Spanish Armada in 1588. For that battle, the English had experimentally equipped ten thousand troops with firearms, with outstanding success. The bow soon became a secondary weapon, and after the last big battle was fought with bows and arrows by the Chinese at Taku in 1860, it became obsolete as a weapon of war. However, some tribes in Africa and South America still use bows and arrows in warfare (as is evidenced by small, slow-flying planes that become "pincushions" over certain jungle areas) and also depend on them as their chief means of taking game and fish.

ARCHERY AS A SPORT

After the decline of the bow as a weapon, archery was forgotten until countries such as England saw its merit as a sport. King Henry VIII was an enthusiastic archer and an ardent bettor who staged large matches and invited wide participation. With the help of this kingly interest, archery became very popular in England, and proficiency in the use of the longbow was common.

Archery was known to the Indians of America when the Pilgrims arrived. The Indians soon gave up their bows and arrows for the more efficient firearms, and so history repeated itself. Archery began as an American sport in 1828 when a group of archers formed the United Bowmen of Philadelphia—which still exists. In 1879, the National Archery Association was founded and yearly national tournaments were begun, the first being held in Chicago.

For more than 100 years, target-archery competition prevailed in America. In 1934, when the NAA held its tournament in Los Angeles, a group of archers interested mainly in bow hunting began agitating for a new kind of game that was suited for off-hand shooting, which was more usable for hunting. Six years later, in 1940, the National Field Archery Association was organized. For ten years competition was restricted to bare-bow shooting, or the use of a single-pin sight. Today, the values of the two main styles of shooting are recognized and tournaments are conducted in two divisions, free style and instinctive.

THE FUTURE OF ARCHERY

The future of the sport looks bright. Archery tackle sales are among the highest of all sporting goods and still rising. People of all ages are taking up the sport. There were 1.7 million bow twangers in 1946, according to the National Recreation Association; in 1960 they numbered more than 4.7 million—up 176 per cent and the trend is still upward. The greatest increase can be seen in the large numbers of newly licensed bow hunters each year. From 1950 to 1966, the number of licensed archery deer hunters in Michigan alone jumped from a few thousand to over forty thousand. Practically every state has special bow seasons which commonly precede the regular deer seasons and usually last much longer. In Michigan, for example, the bow season is five weeks long, while the regular deer season is only fifteen days. Because archery has many merits, it is probable that people of all ages will continue to enjoy it in the years ahead.

Since its inception, the Outdoor Education Project of the American Association for Health, Physical Education, and Recreation has done much to promote archery, primarily in schools and colleges. The numerous workshops conducted throughout the country have enabled thousands to receive training under expert instructors. This effort is expected to continue.

Of special interest to the collegiate archer is the National Collegiate Archery Coaches' Association, which sponsors competition for college men and women on a national basis and selects the All-American Archery team. More details of these organizations are given in Chapter 9.

EQUIPMENT

Archery equipment is commonly called *tackle*. The only tackle absolutely necessary for participation is a bow with string attached and some arrows. However, for comfort and efficiency, an arm guard and finger tab or glove should be worn. To make tackle easier to carry, a quiver should be added to the list.

BOWS

Four main woods are used in making self bows. A *self bow* is made entirely from one piece of material, in contrast to the *laminated bow*, which is made of several pieces of wood or other materials glued together.

Probably the smoothest shooting self-bow wood is yew, a type of cedar that grows in the Pacific Northwest. It is becoming rare, consequently expensive, and market conditions seem to indicate its coming obsolescence. Yew makes a wonderful longbow, especially for target archery, and will not soon be forgotten, for its records have left their imprint for centuries. A yew bow should have some sapwood on the back of the bow, for its elastic quality. The heartwood, better under compression, is used on the belly side.

A good hunting bow can be constructed from osage orange (*Bois d'Arc*), a hardwood tree sometimes called hedgewood, for it is planted in rows to make hedges on many farms ranging from Indiana to Texas.

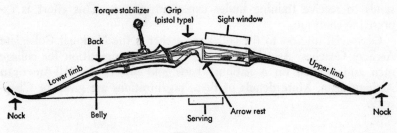

The Bow

6

The tree is thorny and develops a warty, green, nonedible fruit the size of grapefruit. Selection of this wood for bows presents problems in both manufacture and use. The wood is extremely hard, sawing and planing are difficult, so scraping and sanding are often resorted to. The wood is better under *compression* than it is under tension. Consequently, it is better used in the belly of the bow and backed with another wood, such as hickory, or some elastic material. However, good short bows made of osage orange will withstand the abuse they often get under hunting conditions. It does not make an especially good target bow, because it is rather *rough-in-hand*—that is, it tends to kick or recoil.

A third wood commonly used for self bows is lemonwood, named after its creamy, lemon color rather than after the tree it comes from. The tree is *degame*, which grows around the Mediterranean and in Cuba. Even though this wood is imported, it is reasonably priced and is recommended to the beginning hobbyist for his first homemade bow. Although the wood is extremely hard and close grained, it works rather easily. The finished bow may hold up for years of rough use. Lemonwood may be used for target and field or hunting bows. Since it is a hardwood, it has *recoil* tendencies. Also, this wood has a tendency to follow the string, as it is not adept at withstanding stretch or tension. Therefore, better bows can be made by backing lemonwood with a more elastic wood or other material.

Hickory is the fourth most commonly used self-bow wood in the United States. It is fairly abundant, but it is the least desirable of the four woods, because it does not stand compression, is slow in action, has much kick, has poor recovery, and follows the string badly. The best thing that can be said for hickory is that it has excellent stretch qualities; consequently, it can be used successfully to back other bow woods, especially osage orange.

Other self bows are made of solid or hollow fiber glass, steel, and aluminum. Aluminum bows have lost popularity because of the personal danger involved when the bows break. At the present time, fiber glass bows are very popular, especially for schools, camps, beginners, and children. They are durable, have good shooting qualities, stand up well under mistreatment; but they lack that smooth-in-hand quality that the more experienced archer seeks. Low cost and ease of production favor the future of fiber glass bows.

The laminated recurved bow with its beauty in color and design seems to be stealing the hearts of the more experienced archers. It couples gracefulness with a highly efficient, smooth-shooting cast. A most interesting point about these modern bows is the similarity in material and design even when manufactured by different concerns. Most have maple cores and fiber glass backs and bellies. Differences are noted mainly in the color and texture of the fiber glass, the type and color of wood in the handle riser, the length of the bow, the amount of recurve, the weight, and whether the handle rises to the belly or to the back. Handle design favors the pistol grip, which facilitates the use of the extended wrist.

Bow weights vary from 10 to 110 pounds. The ten-pounder might be ideal for the six-year-old, whereas an elephant hunter would use the heavier-weight bow. Bow weight is determined by the number of pounds of pull required to draw the string a specified distance. Most bows are measured at the 28-inch draw length. In Table 1, bow weights for different purposes are suggested.

For best results, left-handed archers should purchase bows with arrow rests on the right side. However, some bows designed for both right and left handers prove satisfactory for camp or school use.

TABLE 1   Bow Weights for Men and Women

Use	*Men*	*Women*
Target archery	30–38 pounds	25–28 pounds
Field Archery	35–42 pounds	25–32 pounds
Hunting* and fishing	42–52 pounds	30–45 pounds

* For bear, moose, lions, elephants, and other tough animals more weight would be necessary.

ARROWS

Arrows are the archer's most important equipment. A good job of scoring can be done with an average bow and excellent arrows, but not with an excellent bow and low-quality arrows. Some qualities to seek in arrows include:

1. *Matched spine—spine* is the stiffness of the shaft as measured by a spine-tester, which supports an arrow at two points while a two-pound weight is applied at the center of the shaft. If arrows having different spine tests are shot from the same bow, they will have varying flights.
2. *Matched for the bow*—for each bow weight there is a proper spine test, and this should be used for best results.

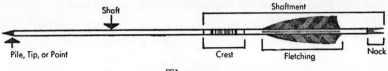

Shaft

Shaftment

Pile, Tip, or Point   Crest   Fletching   Nock

The arrow

3. *Matched weight*—even though shafts may be the same thickness and length, they may vary in weight because of the density of the wood. Using matched-weight arrows is not generally required for beginning archers, but it becomes more important when better hits are desired.
4. *Straight shafts*—an arrow that is not straight has an erratic flight. Straightness is of extreme importance.
5. *Identical length and thickness*—it is dangerous to shoot arrows that are too short since they may strike the bow hand on release or shatter against the inside of the bow. Accuracy is lost if the arrows are too long, too thick, or too heavy.
6. *Identical feathers*—feathers should be evenly spaced and identical in height, length, and shape of trim. Arrows may be straight or spiral *fletched*, right or left sided, or have three or four feathers. Each one in the set should be identical with the others.
7. *Nocks and piles*—these should be securely held and placed straight.
8. *An attractive crest*—this provides good identification of arrows.

A *spinetester*

Wooden arrows are generally made of Port Orford cedar, Norway pine, or birch. Birch is least preferred because of its heavy weight and the fact that arrows made of it become crooked quite readily and are difficult to straighten. Very fine wooden arrows of compressed cedar are now available.

Arrows are also made of aluminum and fiber glass. The expert or even the advanced archer should consider aluminum arrows, because they are light and can be matched perfectly in spine and weight.

Fiber glass arrows have been improved steadily and are now preferred by many archers.

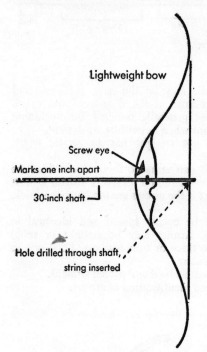

Lightweight bow

Screw eye

Marks one inch apart

30-inch shaft

Hole drilled through shaft, string inserted

Checking arrow length

More important to the beginning archer than the arrow material is arrow length, for if an arrow is too short the archer may be seriously injured through the overdraw, and if it is too long, efficiency is lost. Three ways to check for proper arrow length are: (1) measure arm spread from fingertip to fingertip with arms extended sideways and refer to the arrow-length chart in Table 2; (2) place a yardstick or long arrow against the breastbone (sternum) and extend both arms forward parallel to the floor and have a partner measure or mark the fingertip reach; and (3) attach a 30-inch shaft to the string of a light (15 to 20 pounds) bow (drill a hole through the shaft) and let the pile end run through a screw-eye at the arrow shelf.

TABLE 2 Arrow-Length Chart

Arm Spread (inches)	Arrow Length (inches)
57–59	22–33
60–62	23–24
63–65	24–25
66–68	25–26
69–71	26–27
72–74	27–28
75–77	28–29
Over 77	30

The shaft should be marked at 1-inch intervals so the length of arrow drawn can be read as the archer draws the string and anchors at the appropriate anchor point. This method is the most accurate of those described if the supervisor knows proper form. Such measuring apparatus could be constructed very reasonably.

ARM GUARDS

An arm guard has two main functions: (1) to protect the arm from the slap or recoil of the bowstring and (2) to hold clothing, such as long-sleeved shirts or jackets, close to the arm so the bowstring will not be deflected on its forward progress. The guard should be stiff enough not to curl but not so stiff that it will dig into the junction of hand and wrist.

Arm guard

FINGER PROTECTION

Finger gloves or finger tabs are the commonly used finger protectors. Some sort of protection should be used for two reasons: (1) to protect the releasing fingers from the friction of the bowstring, and (2) to provide a smoother release. The skin rolls toward the fingertips as the string passes over the unprotected, rolled-up flesh, resulting in a rough release; blisters may result from prolonged shooting unless the archer uses finger protection. Some experts have been eliminated in the midst of national tournaments because of blistered fingers, even though protectors were worn.

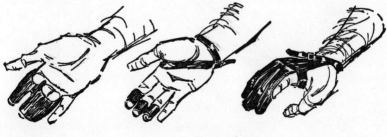

Finger tab   *Finger glove*

Finger gloves provide maximum protection because the three shooting fingers are completely surrounded with leather. Gloves often seem clumsy to the beginner, but with practice, they become an asset. A stiffer leather, such as cordovan, is considered better than a soft cowhide.

A finger tab is a flat piece of leather that goes between the three shooting fingers and the string. Tabs are more reasonably priced than gloves, but they do not give maximum protection. Some users get blisters between the first and second fingers from the arrow nock. Certain experts, however, claim to get slightly more cast from the bow by using a tab, and many target archers prefer tabs, saying they get a smoother release with them.

QUIVERS

Quivers have been designed for all purposes. Ground quivers, back quivers, and hip quivers are most commonly used in target archery.

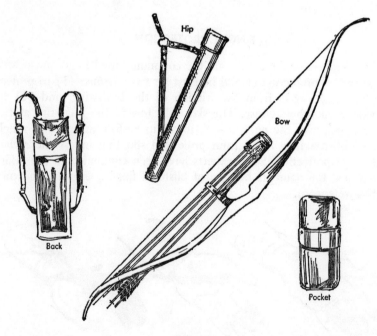

Quivers

Ground quivers, which hold both bow and arrows, have proved to be very satisfactory for group instructional purposes.

Field archers generally use back, hip, or pocket quivers. The pocket quiver seems to be the most favored.

Quivers used in hunting include: center-back quivers, off-the-shoulder back quivers, hip quivers, arm quivers, and bow quivers. Because of the ease of maneuverability and arrow accessibility, the bow quiver is best for hunting most types of game.

CARE OF EQUIPMENT

Inspect all equipment regularly; look especially for damaged arrows. An ounce of prevention is worth a pound of cure. Many little things that go wrong may be repaired before any injury or costly damage occurs.

Bows

1. Store bows in a cool, slightly humid place to preserve flexibility. Hang them vertically on pegs by the string, or in clamps, or preferably lay them horizontally on two pegs. Bows should be unstrung when not in use.
2. Keep bows off the ground; they absorb moisture, which may cause warping or separating of laminations. Also, bows on the ground may be damaged by being stepped on.
3. Refinish wooden bows every year or two, depending on the amount of use and condition of the bow. It is advisable occasionally to apply a good grade of floor wax to the bow.
4. Bow cases help to protect bows in transit or not in use.

Arrows

1. Store arrows in a vertical position so there will be no pressure on the shafts to bend them. Keep them away from moths, which will eat the feathers.
2. If arrows get wet from grass or rain, wipe them before they can absorb moisture. Wooden arrows generally warp when wet.
3. Destroy cracked or splintered wooden arrows so they cannot be used.
4. Nocks and points can be replaced by the novice at negligible cost.
5. Feathers may be replaced. Use fast-drying glues and pins to hold feathers in place while the glue dries, if a fletching jig is not available.
6. Wooden arrows may be straightened by heating the warped area (preferably not over direct flame), rebending it, and allowing it to cool. Aluminum arrows may be straightened with an arrow tube straightener, or an expert may be able to straighten it by hand.

Bowstrings

1. Keep the bowstring well waxed. Use beeswax on all of the string except the center serving, which should be waxed with paraffin.
2. Replace frayed bowstrings before they break.

Accessories

1. Dry leather goods slowly if they get wet. Forced drying by applying heat may crack and shrink the leather.
2. Clean leather with saddle soap.

COST OF EQUIPMENT

Bows vary from $5.00 to $175.00 in cost. A completely satisfactory bow for the beginning adult may be purchased for $20 to $30.

Arrows of wood range in cost from $2.50 to $18.00 a dozen. The beginning adult should get *matched* arrows at around $8.00 to $12.00 a dozen. Fiber glass and aluminum arrows are more costly—$24.00 to $36.00 a dozen.

Arm guards may be made from scrap leather or purchased at prices from $.75 to $3.50.

Finger protectors may be made from scrap leather or purchased at $.35 to $.75 for tabs, while gloves vary from $1.50 to $3.50.

TECHNIQUES
OF PARTICIPATION

The bow must be strung before shooting. There are two acceptable ways of stringing the bow: the pull-push method and the step-in method. In the pull-push method, the bow is pulled by the handle while the upper limb is pushed down and the string slid up simultaneously. The bow, supported thus at three points, will bend evenly without undue stress at any point.

Stringing the bow: (a) *pull-push method;* (b) *step-in method*

In the step-in method, the right leg is put between the string and the belly of the bow (the belly faces forward). The lower end of the bow is placed above the instep of the left foot while the bow handle rests against the back of the thigh. The right hand is used to push the bow forward while the left hand guides the string into the nock. Avoid twisting the bow ends.

A person may be able to shoot a bow and arrow without any instruction, but he will not shoot well unless he knows the proper techniques, and uses them correctly. At first you must think about each fundamental movement as you perform it, but when you know the fundamentals they can become habitual. It is important to begin correctly so that you will not develop bad habits.

THE TEN TECHNIQUES OF TARGET ARCHERY

Although the list of fundamentals could be combined under fewer topics, in the final analysis ten separate techniques are important to mastering the art of shooting. They are: stance, bow arm, nocking, drawing, anchoring, relaxing, aiming, concentrating, releasing, and following through.

1. *Stance*—Stand with a feeling of stability, but avoid stiffness. The feet, about shoulder-width apart, should straddle the shooting line with toes straight ahead. Weight should be evenly distributed, concentrated on neither one foot nor on the toes or heels. The knees and legs should be relaxed and straight; the abdomen should be held in, not allowed to droop forward; the chest should be up and the entire body in good, erect posture with the body's weight resting on its bony structure. The stance should feel comfortable and relaxed. Stand at right angles to the target, the left side facing it, and the head turned toward the target. An open stance helps prevent constant hitting of the bow arm on release.

2. *Bow Arm and Grip*—The bow-arm fundamentals are equally important to the release. It takes only fractions of an inch of bow movement to make many inches of error on the target at twenty yards and beyond. A poor release can be partially balanced out by having a steady bow arm and proper grip. However, poor bow-arm fundamentals cannot be overcome by having a perfect release. Naturally, an archer would want to perfect both bow-arm and release fundamentals.

The grip that seems to be best for most archers when the bow is not too heavy is the extended wrist grip. In this grip the bow handle is pushed with the "V" formed by the junction of the thumb and index finger while the wrist is raised and the fingers straightened and pointed downward. The bow is not gripped at all but rather is supported at maximum arm's length from the body. To keep the bow from falling from the hand at release, wrap the index finger and/or the second finger gently around the back of the handle. A slight pressure to help stabilize the bow may be exerted on the sides of the handle by the thumb and index finger, and the little finger may be lowered to touch the left edge of the bow below the handle, or on the belly. The bones in the wrist should be straight, in alignment, and should "carry the load." Bending the wrist inward, outward, or downward puts musculature into action, which causes wrist movement on release. The bow arm should be fully extended but not locked stiff at the elbow. Rather, the elbow should be turned outward to avoid being hit by the bowstring. The shoulder must be kept down and back. The whole arm should simulate a right-angle brace on a post (the body) and should be held just as steady (without tenseness, however).

Extended wrist grip

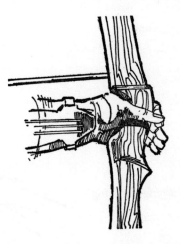

3. *Nocking*—The act of putting the arrow on the string is called *nocking*. To do this, place the bow in a horizontal position so the back of the left hand is pointing up. Take the arrow by the nock, hold it between the thumb and index finger of the right hand, and slide it across the arrow rest (on the left side of the bow) and string with the cock feather up. When the nock end of the arrow reaches the string, remove the index finger from it and reach around and under the string and regrasp the nock. Pull the nock backwards, positioning it onto the

string at the nocking point. The arrow may now be supported against the bow with the index finger of the bow hand until the draw is begun. The arrow should be nocked at a 90-degree angle with the string and top of the arrow rest. The nocking point should be marked with ink, or a nock stop should be constructed on the string.

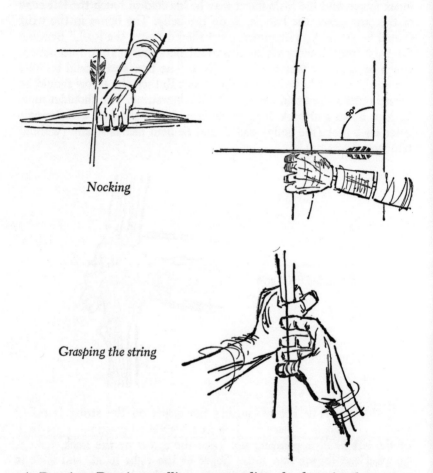

Nocking

Grasping the string

4. *Drawing*—Drawing, pulling, or spreading the bow involves many of the upper body muscles, but in particular the upper arm, shoulder, and upper back muscles. Place the first three fingers of the right hand on the string, having the arrow nock between the first and second

fingers. Position the fingers on the string so they grasp it as far to the tips as possible for comfort and safety. The string may be grasped *at* the first joint, not above, but it is better to have the string nearer the fingertips as this provides a smoother release (less movement involved).

The *fingers* should form a hook and should be relaxed during the draw. Tenseness in the hand must be eliminated; *avoid hooking the hand*. The act of drawing is a simultaneous action of both arms. The bow arm is raised toward the target while the string arm pulls backward. During the draw take a breath of air and hold it.

5. *Anchoring*—Pulling the string to a consistently proper anchor point is of extreme importance. Much variance results from inconsistent anchoring. The best anchor point for sight shooting is under the chin. The string hand should be pulled back so that the index finger comes under the tip of the chin and the string bisects the front of the chin.

The anchor point

The head should be held forward enough so the tip of the nose is also bisected by the string. If you draw the string to the chin and nose each time, you will get a full draw each time and thus develop consistency.

That consistency must be achieved for best results cannot be over-emphasized. Even an eighth of an inch of variance in anchoring will mean a significant error on the target.

6. *Relaxing*—At full draw, you should make a conscious effort to relax. Any athlete will perform better if relaxed rather than tense. The archer at full draw should try to settle down on his bones. That is, body musculature should not be supporting body weight, but the lines of force should go through the bone structure. Any muscles that are tense should be made to relax. Relaxation can be learned and should be practiced. Releasing some of your breath (especially if too much was taken in) may help you relax. Overtensing certain muscles (occasionally between shots) followed by conscious efforts to "let them go" will tend to relax those muscles. This overtensing may be likened to performing isometric exercises.

7. *Aiming*—All methods of aiming can be broadly classified under two headings: (1) bare bow shooting and (2) using aiming devices. Aiming devices, which will be discussed first, include the use of sights

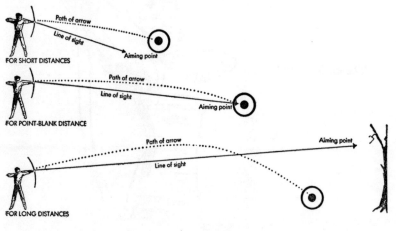

Point-of-aim sighting

and aiming points (point-of-aim). Hundreds of years ago target archers discovered they could shoot better scores by sighting the tips of their arrows onto an object on the ground, or elsewhere, without looking directly at the target. The object, or aiming point, was moved according to the grouping of arrows until the arrows would strike the gold. This method was called *point-of-aim.*

Point-of-aim is still used in target archery but is not as convenient as the "sight method," and is losing its popularity.

The sight-shooting method involves the use of a mechanical device attached to the bow, which is adjustable vertically and horizontally. A sight can be purchased for as little as one dollar or as much as one hundred dollars or more and fastened securely to the bow with screws or tape. It might even consist of a popsicle stick held on with a few rubber bands, or a large-headed pin held by a piece of adhesive tape on the back of the bow. The principle of use is similar in either case.

The sight is usually fastened to the back of the bow with its lower portion about an inch above the arrow rest. The sight pin extends to the left side of the bow and is easily visible as it rides up and down the sight window. To aim with a sight, close the left eye (assuming the right eye is the master eye) and, looking at the sight pin, align it with

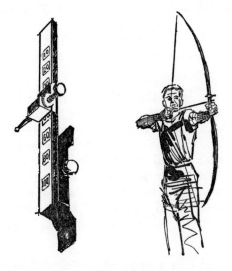

Bow sights

the center of the gold. After shooting several arrows, check the group so that sight adjustments may be made. If your arrows are spread over the target, there probably is inconsistency in performance rather than any fault with the sight's adjustment. Perfect your form first. When the arrows are grouping, adjust the sight according to the group. To make sight adjustments, follow this simple rule: *move the sight in the direction of the error.* If the group is high, move the pin up; if it is low, move the pin down. If the group is right, move the pin right; if it is left, move the pin left. All adjustments on the sight are made in reference to the bow as held in the shooting position.

8. *Concentrating*—Closely related to aiming is the power of concentration. Without this ability an archer will not reach his peak performance. Concentrating involves the ability to put out of your mind any thoughts that are not directly related to shooting a bow. Distracting thoughts may have a physical basis, such as soreness or tiredness; or they may be caused externally, by the wind, sun, or terrain; there may be emotional problems such as worry over examinations, disagreements with others, or concern over finances; or the distraction may have a social basis, such as awareness of being watched or concern over finishing when others do. The archer must devote his entire power of concentration to the sight and center of the target. This ability to concentrate will not be possible, however, if the archer has to think about form. Consequently, form must first be perfected; it must become a habit. *Think about form corrections between shots,* not during the act of shooting.

9. *Releasing*—Releasing is the act of sending the arrow on its way. A great deal of energy is stored in the bow at full draw, and this energy must be directed with initial precision. When you are relaxed in the full draw position, are holding the sight pin steadily on the center of the target, and have achieved full concentration on the task at hand, it is time to release. The archer releases by relaxing the string fingers smoothly, allowing the string to slide over the ends of the glove. Before and after the string is released there should be no voluntary movements of the string hand—that is, the hand should not be snapped to the side, jerked back, or allowed to creep forward.

10. *Follow-through*—The purpose of the follow-through is to ensure the effectiveness of proper fundamentals up to that point. *Follow-*

through means merely holding form for a short time after release. Once the arrow has left the bow, the archer has no effect on its flight; but until the arrow is gone, the archer affects it, especially through his grip, bow-arm movements, and release. Some pointers on follow-through are: keep the anchor point positioned as during release; keep the bow arm extended to the target without allowing the arm to drop or move sideways, or the wrist to twist; maintain the shooting position at least until the arrow hits the target. During the follow-through, study your shot for correct fundamentals. The follow-through in archery may be likened to the "hold" after firing a rifle. The rifle is held on the target for a brief time after the shot is squeezed off.

SHOOTING ERRORS

Regardless of who the archer is there usually comes a time when his score decreases, probably because of erratic form. Many times the individual does not know what mistakes he is making. However, careful self-study or observation by another may soon reveal the answer to the problem. The most common shooting errors and some of their causes follow:

Shooting to the Left

Causes:
1. Natural tendency of most bows to shoot to the left because of their construction. Center-shot bows are less likely to do this.
2. Arrows spined too stiffly for the bow's weight.
3. Sighting with the left eye while shooting right-handed. Close the left eye and use the right.
4. Shooting right-handed but having the left eye as the master eye. Shoot left-handed if the left eye is the master eye and right-handed if the right eye is the master eye.
5. Sight pin set too far to the right.
6. Hunching the bow-arm shoulder. Keep the shoulder down and back.
7. Anchoring to the right of the proper anchor point.
8. Jerking the bow to the left on or before release.
9. Twisting the bow hand outward on or before release, causing the bow to turn left.
10. Left wrist not straight but turned in, causing bow to be angled off to the left.
11. Locking the bow arm on release.
12. Snapping the bow string off to the right on release. Hold anchor.
13. Wind blowing from the right.

Shooting to the Right

Causes:

1. Anchoring to the left of the correct position.
2. Bending the bow arm on or before release. Keep the arm straight.
3. Sight pin set too far to the left.
4. Wind blowing from the left.
5. Outward wrist movement in bow arm on or before release.

Shooting Too High

Causes:

1. Arrow being nocked below the correct nocking point.
2. Opening mouth before or during the release (thus lowering the anchor point).
3. Overdrawing (pulling beyond the normal anchor point).
4. Jerking hand back on release, resulting in extra cast.
5. Anchoring lower than normal anchor point.
6. Sight pin set too low.
7. Leaning back (away from target) on or before release.
8. Overstrung bow (may result in greater cast).
9. Raising bow arm on or before release.
10. Tail wind.
11. Not breathing properly, inhaling just before release.

Shooting Too Low

Causes:

1. Not drawing back to correct anchor point (underdrawing).
2. Letting string hand move forward on or before release (creeping).
3. Pushing or dropping bow arm down on or before release.
4. Arrow nocked above the correct nocking point.
5. Collapsing the bow arm on or before release (loss of cast).
6. Not holding breath properly, exhaling just before release (thus lowering bow arm).
7. Anchoring too high.
8. Holding too long, possibly tiring and letting the bow arm settle slightly.
9. Leaning forward (toward the target) on or before release.
10. Setting sight pin falsely high.
11. Arrows too heavy for bow (loss of speed).
12. Bow too weak (poor cast for longer distances).
13. Bow understrung (loss of efficiency).
14. Hitting clothing, bow arm, or arm guard with the string upon release.
15. Head wind.

Combinations of these errors may cause arrows to hit high and right, for example, or low and left, or any other place on the target. On the other hand, one error might nullify the effect of another and result in a perfect shot. This should not be the archer's goal—to learn to use compensating errors. You should strive to perfect your form and shoot correctly with consistency.

THE TEN TECHNIQUES OF BARE BOW SHOOTING

Bare bow shooting is commonly called *instinctive shooting,* which implies that this ability is somehow inborn in an individual or is a natural aptitude. In reality this is far from the truth; the ability to shoot this way is more dependent upon one's judgment than on instinct. It is a learned ability and a practiced judgment. For lack of a better name, we will call this method the *bare bow method,* because there is no aiming device whatever on the archer's bow.

Bare bow shooting may be better for hunting since sight shooters must know distance to set their sights properly and hunting conditions do not lend themselves well to the setting of sights and the judging of distance. In addition to hunting, and of course bow fishing, bare bow shooting is used in field archery, a game designed to condition and train one for hunting. However, sights can be used very effectively in field archery and satisfactorily in hunting. Many people shoot both ways and it is highly advisable to learn both ways well and eventually to pick the method preferred. Also, an archer sometimes sours on one method if he uses it exclusively, and he will find freshness and a new challenge if he takes up the other style for a time. Both methods have advantages and disadvantages and it is up to the individual finally to judge for himself as to his preference.

The author conducted research on several occasions and concluded that best results are obtained in the learning process by beginning with sight shooting and later learning bare bow shooting. The students who began shooting with sights shot higher scores on the first round and made greater improvement between rounds than those who started shooting using bare bow techniques. Also, when the groups were switched, the students who began shooting with sights immediately learned the bare bow style and made good progress while the others had some difficulty in adjusting to the sights and did not improve as rapidly. However, during your very earliest practice sessions, it is best to spend some time on learning form before you try any method of aiming.

It must be pointed out that for a high score, the sight method is superior. This is easily seen in the scores of archers who shoot in the national tournaments. Shooting on the same courses, the freestyle archers, who use sights, outshoot the bare-bow shooters—even in field archery competition, which is a game especially designed for and by bare-bow archers.

There are a few differences in form between sight and bare bow shooting. The main differences are in aiming and anchor point. Since the techniques of shooting have been described under sight shooting they will only be listed here, but where major differences exist the differences will be explained.

1. *Stance*—(a) Stand relaxed, at right angles to the target. (b) In field archery stand behind the shooting post. (c) Feet should be shoulder-width apart, weight evenly distributed.

2. *Bow arm and grip*—(a) Use the extended wrist grip if the bow is not too heavy, but otherwise use the traditional grip (illustrated).

Traditional grip

(b) Align the bones to form a straight line through the wrist. (c) Do not allow the wrist to move before, during, or just after release. (d) Extend the bow arm fully. (e) Turn the elbow outward. (f) Keep the shoulder down and back. (g) Tilt the bow slightly to the right to get a better view of the target and better eye alignment.

3. *Nocking*—Nock about ⅜ inch above a right angle of the string and top of the arrow rest.

4. *Drawing*—(a) Place string in front of the first joint of the first three fingers and let it slip to the tips of the three fingers as far as possible without losing control. (b) Use the back, shoulder, and upper arm muscles in the draw; spread the arms. (c) Take in a breath of air during the draw and hold it. (d) Begin aiming during the draw. Look intently at the center of the target or a spot on the animal and begin pointing the bow at the intended target.

5. *Anchoring*—(a) Anchor at the back corner of the mouth with the second fingertip and with the hand on the side of the cheek. The anchor point is raised from under the chin (as in sight shooting) to the cheek to get the arrow closer to the eye and thus provide a better feeling of sighting down the arrow (like a gun) when aiming. This higher anchor point also places the arrow directly *under* the right eye, which helps in aligning the arrow on the target. The head should be tilted slightly to the right to ensure that the right eye is directly over the arrow. At the same time, the bow should be tilted to the right somewhere between fifteen and thirty-five degrees (a matter of preference) to get a clearer view of the target and to have better eye alignment. Some archers prefer to keep the bow in the vertical position, which is permissible.

This anchor point is best secured if emphasis (pressure, firmness) is put on the face with the thumb and top of the index finger rather than the fingertips. The first check point in anchoring is the position of the second finger. It should be placed at the back corner of the mouth tugging the lips back slightly as it comes to rest securely but not tightly. The thumb and index finger, which form a "V," should fit around the back of the cheekbone and should be firmly pressed against the cheek to disallow any movements. It is emphasized that pressure against the cheek should be applied with the upper parts of the index finger and thumb rather than with the fingertips. With the hand in this position another easily identifiable check point is the position of the top knuckle of the thumb. It comes to rest comfortably at the ear lobe. Do not release the arrow until the three check points are satisfactorily obtained, namely, the second finger at the back corner of the mouth, the "V" firmly around the cheekbone, and the top knuckle of the thumb at the

*Anchor point
for bare bow shooting*

ear lobe. (b) Anchor at the exact spot consistently. Since facial char-acteristics vary, you may have to vary the suggested anchor point slightly.

6. *Relaxing*—(a) Take in a breath of air during the draw and hold it. (b) If too much air is inhaled, release some. (c) Settle down at full

draw. Relax musculature in legs and arms. Rest on the bones of the body. (d) Consciously relax the musculature of the body.

7. *Aiming*—Aiming while shooting with a bare bow is quite a departure from using a bow sight. Keep both eyes open rather than closing one eye. This affords a better perspective, a bigger field of vision, and better depth perception. In other words, the target will stand out more clearly and you can judge the distance to the target more accurately. Occasionally, however, there will be an individual who will be better off to close one eye because of some characteristic of vision.

The difficulty of shooting bare bow lies in the fact that every shot requires 100 per cent effort and concentration; there are no mechanical aids, no formulas, no sure-fire techniques. Each shot is a complete challenge, and the archer who cannot give his all usually fails unless luck is with him.

The first important point in bare bow aiming is to *pick a spot* at which to aim. On the standard field-archery target the center spot is well defined and quite small. On the standard target-archery face, however, the gold center is large (9 inches), and at distances up to 40 yards the exact center of the gold should be aimed at to focus the eyes on something small. In game hunting, a spot must be selected on the animal (usually the heart area) to avoid looking at the entire animal. It is extremely important to be able to pick a focusing spot on any target. During the draw, begin to look at the spot; at full draw, with the arrow anchored properly under the right eye, concentrate intensely on the spot. Intently stare and focus on the spot only; see in the field of vision secondarily the entire target, the bow, arrow, and bow arm.

Do not look directly at any of the things that are in the field of vision —only at the exact spot to be hit. By looking at the intended target, the archer points the bow at it automatically, just as if he were pointing the index finger at something that the eyes are looking at. It is not necessary to look at the finger when pointing at something—only at the object. This process can also be compared to throwing a ball. The thrower looks only at the target (the glove or whatever) and throws to it without actually looking at his hand or the ball. He learns by practicing how low or high, or how hard or easy to deliver the ball. This is exactly what the bare-bow archer must learn to do. He needn't be concerned with how hard or easy to shoot (because each shot should be the same full draw), but he needs to learn how high or low to hold depending on the distance to the target. This is the difficult part of bare-bow shooting. It must be learned through practice and understanding of the equipment being used. Naturally, the longer distances afford the most difficulty in making the elevation adjustment. At long distances, hold the bow hand above the target; at short distances, hold the hand below the target. There is no rule to state how high or low to hold. It depends on the bow's weight, the arrows, the anchor point, and other such variables. If arrows are grouping on the target in a vertical line pattern, it indicates that releases are good but that difficulty is being encountered in elevation judgment. If arrows are spread laterally, it may indicate good elevation judgment, but poor releases, bow hand movements, or other form mistakes.

Some archers find it helps their aim to look at the distance relationship, or gap, between the arrow tip and the center of the target or some other part of the target. This may be called the *gap* method of aiming. If you take the gap relationship between the center of the target and the arrow tip *before* the draw, it would be called the *pre-gap* method. Either of these aiming methods may be used to learn aiming or to supplement the bare bow method.

The gap and pre-gap methods are similar to point-of-aim, since the archer sights over the tip of his arrow in both. The main difference lies in the fact that you should look at the center of the target after establishing the gap, rather than keeping your sight over the tip of the arrow as in point-of-aim.

8. *Concentrating*—If the fundamentals of shooting bare-bow style are mastered, concentration becomes the most important aspect of shooting. The importance of the ability to focus on a spot and forget everything else cannot be overemphasized. Look at the spot so intently as to become nearly self-hypnotized. Upon release the arrow slips away and seems to fly down a tube pointed at mid-center. Both eyes must be trained to focus unwaveringly at a small spot (in the case of a rabbit sitting at three yards it may be a certain hair near the heart area); nothing must be allowed to interfere with the shot at hand, not even thinking about getting a smooth release. Form must be automatic before intense concentration is possible. In the final analysis, you will probably become as skilled as your concentration powers permit. This presupposes that form is perfected and good equipment is used.

9. *Releasing*—(a) Let the string slip off the ends of the fingers as you release them. (b) Do not make any movements before, during, or after release that may affect the flight of the arrow. (c) The "dead" release is recommended—do not let the hand slide back on release. The sliding release may be permissible for experts, but it seems to be too difficult for beginners.

10. *Follow-through*—(a) Maintain the anchor point for a few moments after release. (b) Keep the bow arm extended and pointing at the target for a few moments after release. (c) Do not let the wrist of the bow arm twist before, during, or after release. (d) Study the shot— why was it good or bad? (e) If you made any mistakes, implant the proper form in mind before the next shot. Think the correct way of shooting and then do it that way on the *next* shot.

RULES

The rules of archery may be divided into two categories—those dealing with safety of personnel or equipment and those concerned with competition or participation. Since there is an element of danger in the use of bows and arrows, the safety rules should be strictly kept. If they are, the sport will be perfectly safe and enjoyable for all concerned.

SAFETY RULES AND PRECAUTIONS

1. Never release the bowstring without an arrow on it. The shock sometimes breaks the bow or the string.
2. Limber a bow up with several short draws before pulling it to full draw. This is especially important if the bow has been idle for some time or if the temperature is radically different from that in which the bow was stored.
3. Check to see that the distance between bow handle and string is proper. This distance is a *fistmele*, or that distance recommended by the manufacturer. Make necessary adjustments by taking the string off the bow and twisting or untwisting it. Too little distance results in wrist slap; too great a distance may result in a broken bow. Neither is good for the bow's efficiency.
4. Before shooting, check arrows for cracks, chrysals, splinters, loose feathers, loose nocks or points, glue deposits, and for straightness. Do not shoot damaged arrows. Break cracked or split arrows so they can't be shot.
5. Be sure arrows are long enough. Never draw an arrow past the bow handle between string and belly. If the correct length cannot be had, it is safer to have slightly longer arrows rather than shorter ones.
6. Check the bow for chrysals, cracks, splits, or scratches, and determine beforehand if there is danger of breakage.
7. Check the string before shooting for frays, broken strands, and loose serving. Repair or replace the string before breakage occurs.
8. A bow is designed and built to bend one way only, be careful not to string it backward.
9. Never shoot an arrow straight up in the air. This is very dangerous and the arrow often goes out of sight and wind currents will make it extremely difficult to know where the arrow will land.

10. Never point an "armed" bow at a person.
11. Wear simple clothing. Avoid fancy buttons, big pockets, jewelry, beads, sorority or fraternity pins, and so on, because the bowstring often catches on such things, and the arrow is deflected; these things may be pulled off by the string and lost.
12. Keep the bow-arm elbow turned out to avoid hitting it with the bowstring.
13. Be sure to wear an arm guard and finger tab or glove. Welts or blisters may develop without this needed protection.
14. Do not shoot if anyone is near the target, behind it, or between you and the target.
15. When pulling arrows from the target, make sure no one is immediately in front of the target, to avoid the possibility of accident as the arrows are removed. Serious injury to the eyes of others could result during the arrow withdrawal process.
16. To withdraw the arrow, place one hand against the target, palm out, with the arrow between the first and second fingers; with the other hand, grasp the arrow close to the target and pull it out at the same angle it went in.
17. When arrows become buried in the grass, pull them forward from the pile end to avoid feather damage.
18. Arrows with feathers partially driven into the target should be pulled through from behind the target, pile first.
19. Always be conscious of the possible danger of bows and arrows.

SIMPLIFIED RULES OF COMPETITION AND PARTICIPATION IN TARGET ARCHERY

1. Straddle the shooting line.
2. Wait for a signal from the field captain to begin shooting.
3. Shoot six arrows only.
4. Step back after shooting an end and stay back until all archers have finished.
5. Wait for a signal from the field captain to retrieve arrows.
6. All archers shoot at the same time and retrieve at the same time.
7. In target archery, shoot only at the target.
8. An arrow that falls from the bow that can be reached with the aid of the bow may be shot again. If it can't be reached without moving, it is considered shot and counts zero.
9. If tackle breaks during shooting, the arrow is considered shot.
10. Six arrows constitute an "end." A round is made up of a number of ends at several (usually three) different ranges (or distances).

11. Score—the target consists of five concentric rings. The yellow inner circle (gold) counts nine points; the red ring counts seven; the blue, five; the black, three; and the white, one.
12. An arrow that cuts a line between two colors counts the higher value.
13. An arrow that passes through the scoring face so that it is not visible from the front shall count seven at 60 yards or less, and five for ranges beyond 60 yards. Arrows passing completely through the target, if witnessed, are scored in the same manner.
14. An arrow that hits in the petti-coat has no scoring value. The petticoat includes the outer black line around the white ring and the area outside of this ring.

The target

15. An arrow that rebounds from the scoring face, if witnessed, shall score the same as a pass-through.
16. An arrow that hits a target other than the one shot at shall score as a miss.
17. If more than six arrows are shot in one end, only the lowest six shall score.
18. In tournament shooting, usually groups of four people shoot at each target. One is the target captain who calls the value of each arrow as he pulls it from the target. Its value shall be recorded independently by two contestants acting as scorers, normally the next two assigned to the target. Scorers should check results after each end to avoid errors. Each archer is individually responsible for seeing that his arrows are called correctly and entered properly on the score card.
19. Scores are recorded by listing the highest first and proceeding to the lowest. Each score must be recorded in the space provided on the scoring card. Zero is indicated for misses or for hits outside the scoring face.
20. The longest distance in a round is shot first, progressing to the shortest.
21. In case of a tie, the highest score at the longest distance is the winner.
22. In a tournament, there is no practice allowed between the various ranges which constitute the round.
23. The center of the gold should be 51 inches from the ground.
24. An arrow must be left in the target until scored.
25. Arrows must bear a distinctive crest so that they can be identified easily.

26. If the point-of-aim method of shooting is used, the aiming point may not be placed more than 6 inches above the ground. Any type of sight attached to the bow may be used.
27. Any type of bow except a crossbow may be used in competition. Crossbow enthusiasts often stage separate tournaments.
28. Presiding officials in tournaments are the *Field Captain*, for men, and the *Lady Paramount*, for ladies.
29. Classifications of archers:
    Men
    Women
    Intermediate boys and girls (fifteen to seventeen years old)
    Junior boys and girls (twelve to fourteen years old)
    Beginner boys and girls, or Cadets (eleven years and under)
30. Some of the common rounds and their users include:

    A. The Columbia Round—for women, intermediate girls, and junior girls (this round works well for college men beginners, and could be used for high school boys):
       four ends at 50 yards;
       four ends at 40 yards;
       four ends at 30 yards.

    B. The American Round—for men and women, intermediate boys and girls:
       five ends at 60 yards;
       five ends at 50 yards;
       five ends at 40 yards.

    C. The National Round—for women and intermediate girls:
       eight ends at 60 yards;
       four ends at 50 yards.

    D. The Metropolitan Round—for women:
       five ends at 60 yards;
       five ends at 50 yards;
       five ends at 40 yards;
       five ends at 30 yards.

    E. The Metropolitan Round—for men:
       five ends at 100 yards;
       five ends at 80 yards;
       five ends at 60 yards;
       five ends at 50 yards;
       five ends at 40 yards.

    F. The York Round—for men (one of the oldest):
       twelve ends at 100 yards;
       eight ends at 80 yards;
       four ends at 60 yards.

G. The Chicago Round—recommended for indoor tournaments. Use a 16-inch five-ring target face:
fifteen ends at 20 yards.

H. Junior Columbia—for junior girls or all beginners under twelve:
four ends at 40 yards;
four ends at 30 yards;
four ends at 20 yards.

I. Junior American—for junior boys:
five ends at 50 yards;
five ends at 40 yards;
five ends at 30 yards.

J. Junior Metropolitan—for juniors:
five ends at 40 yards;
five ends at 30 yards;
five ends at 20 yards.

K. Cadet American—for boys and girls under eleven years:
fifteen arrows at 30 yards;
fifteen arrows at 20 yards.

L. Operation Archery Round (suitable for all beginners). The nice feature of this round is the variety of shooting it offers (distances and sizes of targets). Each part is worth 150 points, so 300 is perfect:
Part 1—Modified Flint Round (score 5 and 3):
four arrows at 17 yards—18-inch face;
four arrows at 20 feet—12-inch face;
four arrows at 20 yards—18-inch face;
four arrows at 14 yards—12-inch face;
four arrows at 15 yards—18-inch face;
four arrows at 10 yards—12-inch face;
one arrow from each: 20 yards, 17 yards, 15 yards, 14 yards, 10 yards, 20 feet—18-inch face.

Part 2—Modified Chicago Round (score 5, 4, 3, 2, 1):
six ends of five arrows each at 20 yards—36-inch face.

SIMPLIFIED RULES FOR FIELD ARCHERY

1. Archers shoot in groups of four. One is the target captain who pulls the arrows and calls the score while the scorer records the scores.
2. The course should be so constructed that it is safe to be shooting at all targets simultaneously without endangering any of the participants.
3. The danger signal is "timber."
4. Be courteous while others shoot. Avoid loud talking and other distractions that may bother competitors.

5. Stand behind the shooting stake when addressing the target and shoot four arrows at the target if it is a one-position shot. If it is a four-position shot, shoot one arrow from each position. The four positions may be either a fan-shape, or a walk-up type, which gets progressively closer to the target on each shot.
6. If archers are looking for stray arrows behind the target, one archer should remain at the target or a bow should be left standing across the target face. The succeeding archers should not shoot until all archers have left.

Field archery target

7. Scoring—The center circle of white including the small black spot scores five while the outer black circle counts three. Arrows that bisect a line count the higher value. Arrows that penetrate the target scoring face so the nocks are not visible from the front score three. Each score must be recorded on the score sheet with the highest scores first. All misses are listed as zeros.
8. The Flint Round is recommended for beginners. See Table 3 for the course set-up. Shoot these seven targets twice.

TABLE 3   Course for the Flint Round

Target 1	25 yards	12-inch face
Target 2	20 feet	6-inch face
Target 3	30 yards	12-inch face
Target 4	15 yards	6-inch face
Target 5	20 yards	12-inch face
Target 6	10 yards	6-inch face
Target 7	30, 25, 20, 15 yards (walk-up, one shot from each post)	12-inch face

9. The NFAA round. Fourteen targets may form a national field archery course. The course should be shot twice for a full round, or a 28-target course may be constructed. See Table 4.

TABLE 4   Course for the NFAA Round

Target 1	50 yards	18-inch face
Target 2	20 yards	12-inch face
Target 3	30 yards	12-inch face
Target 4	60 yards	24-inch face
Target 5	55 yards	24-inch face
Target 6	40 yards	18-inch face
Target 7	15 yards	12-inch face
Target 8	65 yards	24-inch face
Target 9	35, 30, 25, 20 feet (walk-up)	6-inch face
Target 10	25 yards	12-inch face
Target 11	45, 40, 35, 30 yards (walk-up)	18-inch face
Target 12	35 yards (fan)	12-inch face
Target 13	45 yards	18-inch face
Target 14	80, 70, 60, 50 yards (walk-up)	24-inch face

OTHER ARCHERY GAMES

Archery Golf

In some parts of the country archery golf is a popular game. It is played on a golf course. One bow and three arrows may be used: the flight arrow, the approach arrow, and the putting arrow, which may be a flu-flu. The cup is a 4-inch disc or ball placed near the green cup. The object of the game is to go around the course in as few shots as possible. Nine under golf par for nine holes is considered good archery-golf par. The game may easily be improvised for any large open area and could be played most of the year around.

Wand Shooting

This game consists of shooting thirty-six arrows at a wand 2 inches wide and 6 feet long. Balsa wood is best because it holds arrows and minimizes rebounds. Men shoot from 100 yards and women from 60 yards. The wand or stripe could be made of paper and put on a regular target and the distances could be modified. Only those arrows count as hits which are actually embedded in the wand, or which are witnessed rebounds.

Clout Shooting

Clouts consists of shooting at a 48-foot-diameter target laid out on the ground in concentric circles like a 48-inch target, with like values for scoring. Thirty-six arrows are shot from 180 yards for men; women shoot the same number of arrows from 140 or 120 yards. A flag is used to mark the center of the target.

Roving Archery

Rovers pick targets at random. Each archer shoots one shot. A direct hit or the closest to a hit scores one point. The point winner selects the next target. Distances are varied and targets may include clumps of grass, stumps, paper, and so on. The player with the highest number of points is the winner.

6 SELF-IMPROVEMENT AND TRAINING

All athletes know that they must train to achieve success in their sports. Likewise in archery, you must pursue a type of training program, whether to become highly skilled or merely to learn to shoot properly. The following eight principles of training will help you understand yourself in archery while you are a beginner and help you to improve when you become an advanced archer.

Overload—Some work or stress must occur. To become an archer, you must train yourself in the act of pulling the bow and releasing arrows. This might be considered work, or overload, but without it you cannot become an archer. Overload should be applied gradually during adaptation. Avoid excessive fatigue and take frequent rest periods at first; duration of work may be increased gradually.

Intensity—It is the intensity of training—not the duration—that produces most rapid improvement. If you practice seriously and concentrate on your shots, you will accomplish more in thirty minutes than you will in an hour of lackadaisical practice. This does not mean to shoot fast but that you should be intent on what you are doing.

Specificity—You get exactly what you train for. If you train to lift heavy weights, you will develop strength. If you train to move the entire body over long distances or for a great number of repetitions in a certain activity, you will develop endurance. If you practice shooting a bow in a certain way, you will learn to shoot it *that* way. Many factors influence the way a person actually learns to shoot. Some of these are watching demonstrations, listening to expert advice, looking at movies, reading about it, thinking about it. However, the exact way the archer performs at a given time is the way he has learned. This is not to say that changes can never be made but to reemphasize the specificity of training. An archer who learns to shoot with a sight only, has not learned to shoot without a sight, and vice versa. To shoot the other way requires further training of the exact style desired. *You shoot the way you trained to shoot.*

Retrogression—During training there will be times when improvement does not show and when your performance actually drops below normal. This retrogression may occur at different times, but it often occurs early in training after a short burst of initial improvement or after a change in training routine. The retrogression may indicate a period when the body is mobilizing its resources to adapt to the situation. Beginners who avoid feeling discouraged and continue to practice properly soon see improvement again. Even advanced archers sometimes fall into a slump or retrogress when they try something new.

Repetition—Short periods of systematic repetition produce muscular efficiency. If beginning practice is too long, fatigue sets in, steadiness decreases, and errors creep in. When you are tired, it is next to impossible to shoot properly, and poor form is inevitable if you practice when fatigued. In early learning it is better to practice in short frequent sessions while you are concentrating on form. After form is learned, longer periods of practice may be beneficial.

Motivation—Having goals and objectives hastens success. The objectives you set for yourself in archery will give you the drive, or motivation, to succeed. A person may begin the sport because of curiosity to learn, he may want to learn to hunt, or he may wish to become a competitive archer. Whatever your reason, establish goals that are attainable. As you reach one goal successfully it will add impetus to continue on toward your next goal. As momentum picks up, motivation is enhanced and more success results. There are many goals an archer can strive for. A few are: having fun, hitting the bullseye, getting a higher score, shooting in a tournament, shooting a wild animal, or being a champion.

Individual differences—Each person responds uniquely to training. Some of the factors that affect responses to training are: body type—some types respond better to training than others; physical fitness level—alertness, strength, endurance, agility, coordination all affect learning efficiency; past physical activities—the person who has trained will respond better than one who has never trained; physical-psychological interrelationship—your perception of your own ability affects the rate and quality of learning.

Maintenance—It is easier to maintain skill than to attain it. You cannot reach your peak in archery without frequent intensive training. But after you reach a desired level of skill, it is easier to stay there than it was to get there. Less frequent practice periods will keep you at that level but will not necessarily bring improvement. Each person must determine for himself how often he should train to maintain a certain level.

SPECIFIC EXERCISES FOR ARCHERY

Even though archery does not demand so much physically as some other activities, it behooves the archer to have a fair level of fitness. The following exercises are recommended to supplement actual shooting practice:

1. Push ups—to develop the triceps used in drawing and in keeping the bow arm straight.
2. Pull-ups or arm curls—to develop the biceps and pectorals used in the draw.
3. Lateral arm raises with resistance—to develop the rhomboid (back) muscles used principally at the end of the draw. Method: lie on bench in prone position, weights in hands. Start lift from floor raising upward as high as possible, lower to floor and repeat.
4. Sit-ups with bent legs—to develop abdominal musculature. These muscles are extremely important in fitness. They help posture, circulation, and respiration.
5. Running or fast walking and hiking—to develop the legs and the cardiovascular/respiratory system. Such activity builds the endurance essential to complete a task without undue fatigue.

HOW TO BEGIN A SHOOTING PROGRAM

1. Get proper well-fitting equipment.
2. Study fundamentals, watch experts, see visual aids, get proper instruction.
3. Start shooting without a target face at five to ten yards. Stay here for quite awhile.
4. Concentrate on form, perform correctly from the beginning, restudy fundamentals, think about how to perform, don't be score conscious yet. Use a target face after form is well-developed. Keep reviewing form and have experts check it, correct any faults immediately.
5. Gradually increase distance shot. More emphasis can be placed on aiming and aiming devices as you increase distance.
6. Practice frequently for short periods of time, two one-half hour periods daily at first would be better than one two-hour period. Later practice periods may be increased as fitness and skill develop.
7. After you have perfected form and aiming, it only takes concentration to become a champion. Good luck.

GLOSSARY

This glossary includes only those terms currently used. It is not intended to include every term that has had significance in the field of archery.

Arm guard: A device worn on the forepart of the bow arm to protect the arm and wrist from the slap and recoil of the bowstring.

Arrow rest: The part of the bow handle or bow that forms a shelf to hold the arrow as it rides across the bow.

Back: The side of a bow which is away from the archer as he is shooting; the part most under tension during the draw.

Backed bow: A bow that has been strengthened or protected by some material glued to the back, such as rawhide, wood with high tensile strength, fiber glass, bamboo, or metal.

Belly or face: The inside of the bow facing the archer; the part that is compressed during the draw, or the string side.

Bending the bow, bracing the bow, stringing the bow: Terms used to describe the process of placing the bowstring into the bow notches to ready it for shooting.

Blunt: An arrow with a blunt tip instead of a pointed one, used primarily for small-game hunting. The tip may be metal, rubber, or plastic.

Bowman: Another term for an archer, one who engages in shooting bows and arrows.

Bow stave: A piece of cut wood from which a bow is made.

Bowyer: A person who makes archery tackle, especially bows.

Broadhead: A tip used on hunting arrows; there are various designs, but all are essentially designed with sharp cutting edges to permit deep penetration to kill game by hemorrhage.

Butt or target: A backstop to halt arrows; it may be baled straw or excelsior, woven targets of straw or grasses, or plastic foam.

Cast: The ability of a bow to shoot an arrow; the distance a bow can shoot; or the speed at which the bow delivers arrows.

Chrysal: Compression fracture of fibers usually showing as a line across the belly of a self bow. Chrysals may be seen on arrows also, especially if they have been stepped on.

Clout shooting: Shooting at a 48-foot-diameter target laid out on the ground in concentric circles. Men shoot from 180 yards and women from 120 or 140 yards.

Cock feather: The feather at right angles to the nock. It should be perpendicular to the bow when the arrow is being shot.

Composite bow: A bow made of two or more materials, such as wood and fiber glass.

Creep: To allow the string hand to move forward just before or during the release, resulting in a loss of cast.

Crest: Colored marks on the arrow used for identification.

Draw, pull, spread: The act of pulling the bowstring the proper distance, to the anchor point. *Draw* and *pull* also refer to the act of removing the arrows from the target.

End: Six arrows shot in succession.

Eye, loop: The bend in the ends of a bowstring to secure it to the bow.

Field arrow: An arrow used mostly in field archery. It is usually more rugged than a target arrow, having bigger vanes and a heavier, longer pile or tip.

Field captain: Man on the target range in charge of a tournament.

Finger tab, finger cot, finger stall, finger tip, finger glove: Leather device used for the three shooting or string fingers to protect them from the bowstring and also to give a smoother release.

Fistmele: The distance between the base of the hand and the tip of the extended thumb (about 6 or 7 inches). It is the desired distance between the bow handle and the string and should be checked before using the bow each session. Follow the bow manufacturer's specifications whenever given.

Fletching: The feathers on an arrow, usually three or four.

Flight arrow: A long, thin, light arrow, usually barreled with small vanes and pile, used in distance shooting.

Flight shooting: Shooting an arrow for maximum distance. Arrows have been shot over one-half mile.

Flu-Flu: Extra large feathers on an arrow to slow it down rapidly—used in archery games or hunting small game.

Follow the string: An expression used to explain the set a bow takes toward the string after being used. A good bow should not follow the string to any appreciable degree.

Footed arrow: An arrow that has a piece of hardwood spliced into the foreshaft to give it more weight, strength, and better balance.

Grip: The handle of a bow.

Ground quiver: A rod of metal stuck into the ground, shaped to hold arrows and bows while on the range.

Group: Arrows in the target in close proximity.

Hand: Shooting four arrows in field archery.

Head, tip, point, pile: The "business end" of the arrow, usually made of brass, steel, or aluminum.

Hen feathers: The two feathers on an arrow paralleling the nock.

Hit: A successful shot within the target scoring face.

Holding: Keeping an arrow at full draw while aiming. The hold should be for two or three seconds.

Instinctive shooting: Aiming and shooting a bow without the aid of a point of aim, bow sight, or other mechanical means. It is better described as a learned judgment rather than an instinct. Within this text it is called the *bare bow method* of shooting.

Jerking: Abruptly moving the string hand on release.

Kick: The recoil of a bow after it is shot.

Lady paramount: Woman on the range in charge of a tournament.

Limbs: The two arms of a bow, one above and one below the handle.

Longbow: A hand bow 5 or more feet in length.

Loose, release: The act of letting the string slip from the fingertips to shoot the arrow.

Nock: The groove on the end of an arrow into which the string fits. Also the notches on either end of a bow which hold the string. To place an arrow on the string is "nocking an arrow."

Nocking point: The position on the string where the arrow is placed.

Overbowed: Using a bow that is too heavy for the individual.

Overdraw: To pull an arrow past the handle of the bow or to use a longer arrow than the bow was designed to handle safely.

Overstrung: The string being too short for the bow, more than a fistmele between bow handle and string.

Petticoat: The black rim and all the target face outside the white; an arrow in the petticoat counts as a miss.

Point-blank range: The distance at which the aiming point is at the center of the gold, while using the point-of-aim method of shooting.

Point-of-aim: A method of aiming using an aiming point to sight upon with the tip of the arrow to aid the archer in hitting the target.

Quiver: A receptacle for holding arrows. Types of quivers include: back, hip, bow, leg, arm, and ground.

Range: The distance to be shot; or the place where shooting is done.

Range finder: A device to aid the archer in relocating the position of his aiming point.

Recurved bow: A bow with tips that curve back in a graceful arc.

Reflexed bow: A bow that bends backward in its entirety when unstrung, but does not necessarily have recurved ends. Bows may be recurved and reflexed.

Release: To let the string slip off the fingertips; to shoot the arrow.

Round: Shooting a prescribed number of ends or hands at prescribed distances.

Roving: Shooting at random targets such as stumps, paper, clumps of grass, and so on, with unknown and varying distances; good practice for hunting.

Scattered: Describes arrows that are in different places on the target rather than grouped.

Self arrow: An arrow of a single piece of wood, in contrast to a footed arrow.

Self bow: A bow made of one kind of wood, in contrast to a composite bow.

Serving: The winding of string around the center of a bowstring and its loops to protect it from wear by the fingers, arrow nock, and bow nocks.

Shaft: The dowel of which an arrow is made.

Shaftment: That portion of the arrow from the nock through the crest.

Shooting line: The line the target archer straddles while shooting at targets.

Spine: The stiffness-flexibility combination of an arrow. Arrows should be spined for the weight of the bow in which they are used.

Stagger: The erratic flight of an arrow.

Tackle: The equipment used by an archer.

Target face: The painted part of a target including the gold and the other concentric rings.

Tassel: Cloth with which to wipe arrows that become wet or soiled.

Throwaways: Arrows no longer good for competition, but usable when chance of their being broken or lost is great.

Timber: Term used in field archery to warn others that an arrow is being shot; same as "fore" in golf.

Timber hitch: A kind of knot used to tie the lower end of a single-looped string to the bow.

Toxophilite: One who loves, studies, and practices archery.

Trajectory: The path of an arrow in flight.

Underbowed: Using a bow that is too light for the archer.

Understrung: Describes a bow having a string too long; less than a fistmele between handle and string.

Vane: Feather on an arrow.

Wand shooting: Shooting at a slat 2 inches wide and 6 feet high from a long distance.

Weight: The number of pounds pull required to pull a bow the correct arrow length. The actual weight of an arrow in grains.

Weight in hand: The avoirdupois weight of a bow.

Wobble: The erratic action of an arrow in flight.

SELF-TESTING AND EVALUATION

In archery, perhaps more than in most sports, form plays a significant role. Often the archer is not aware of his own mistakes in form. Therefore, it will help to work with an expert instructor or an experienced archer, or to analyze yourself using the following checklist. Better still, do all three.

ARCHERY FORM EVALUATION CHECKLIST

Name of Archer _____ Date _____

Name of Evaluator _____ Type of Shooting _____

Check (√) each item if it is correctly executed. Mark it (X) if incorrect and note in the space provided what is wrong or what needs to be done to improve.

1. Stance

____A. Feet parallel, shoulder width apart. _____
____B. Weight evenly distributed (astride shooting line in target archery, behind post in field archery). _____
____C. Body erect, abdomen flat, weight supported by bones, relaxed. _____

2. Grip and Bow Arm

____A. Extended wrist grip used, relaxed fingers. _____
____B. Upper edge of index finger just below the arrow rest. _____
____C. Wrist straight. _____
____D. Elbow pointing outward, arm not locked stiff _____
____E. Shoulder level, not hunched or turned in. _____
____F. No wrist movement before, during, or immediately following the release. _____
____G. Bow arm steady. _____

47

3. Nocking

_____A. Arrow nocked consistently at a 90° angle with the string, bisecting at the arrow rest for sight shooting. Arrow nocked ⅜" above a 90° angle for bare bow shooting. _____

_____B. Cock feather out. _____

4. Drawing

_____A. String held near the fingertips with three fingers. _____

_____B. *Fingers only* form a hook, hand is straight and relaxed, thumb in palm. _____

_____C. Forearm, wrist, and hand form a continuous line with the arrow. _____

_____D. Full draw on each shot. _____

_____E. Relaxation evident. _____

_____F. Breath taken and held. _____

5. Anchoring

_____A. Anchor point (under chin for sight shooting; at corner of mouth for bare bow shooting) consistently the same. _____

_____B. String cuts across center of chin, lips, and nose in sight shooting, at side of nose in bare bow shooting. _____

_____C. Head remains level and turned fully toward the target. _____

_____D. Mouth closed, chin in normal position. _____

6. Relaxing

_____A. Body weight settled onto the bones rather than supported tensely by musculature. _____

_____B. Good breath control evident. _____

_____C. Conscious effort to relax musculature evident. _____

7. Aiming

_____A. Aim for two or three seconds *after* coming to full draw. _____

_____B. Left eye closed (for most archers) when using sight; both eyes open (for most archers) when bare bow shooting. _____

_____C. Eyes function properly, master eye is known. _____

8. Concentrating

_____A. Archer seems to have mastered any physical or emotional problems and devotes all his attention to hitting the target. _____

_____B. Form is perfected, so concentration can be obtained without the problem of trying to correct any aspect of form. _____

9. Releasing

_____A. Anchor point remains solid before, during, and immediately after release. _____

_____B. The string slips off the fingertips. _____

10. Following through

_____A. No string hand movements that adversely affect the arrow's flight. _____

_____B. No unwarranted grip and bow arm movements. _____

_____C. Shooting position is held until the arrow hits the target. _____

ARCHERY-KNOWLEDGE QUESTIONS

The following questions should be answered to ensure a well-rounded knowledge of archery.

1. What are the main types of woods used in making bows?
2. What woods are used in making arrows?
3. Name the parts of a bow.
4. Name the parts of an arrow.
5. How is arrow length determined?
6. What is meant by *spine?*
7. What is the size of an official target archery face? Give scoring values.
8. How many archers shoot at each target in a tournament? What are their titles and duties?
9. What is the title of the person in charge of a tournament?
10. What is meant by *cast?*
11. What is the value of a pass-through arrow on a 48-inch face?
12. What does *fistmele* mean?
13. How is the score recorded?
14. What does *creeping* mean?
15. What are the ten fundamental techniques of shooting? Describe each.

16. How is a bow sight used?
17. How is a single-looped bowstring attached to a bow?
18. What causes arrows to hit to the left?
19. What causes arrows to hit too low?
20. What are the safety rules in archery?

COLUMBIA AND FLINT ROUND STANDARDS

TABLE 5   Percentile Scores for Men and Women—Columbia and Junior Columbia Rounds*

Percentile Rank	Columbia Round		Jr. Columbia Round
	Men	Women	Women
100	560	505	505
90	400	245	305
80	360	215	255
70	340	185	235
60	310	165	215
50	290	145	195
40	270	135	175
30	250	125	155
20	230	105	135
10	190	75	105
0	100	20	20

* N = 1259 for men, 697 for women in the Columbia Round; N = 1740 for women in the Junior Columbia Round.

TABLE 6   Field Archery Scores—Flint Round* (Percentile Rankings)

Men's Score	Percentile	Women's Score
184	100	70
122	90	53
109	80	46
99	70	32
87	60	30
79	50	26
68	40	25
61	30	15
55	20	12
40	10	9
20	0	3

* N= 153 for men, 25 for women.

It usually helps to know how your performance rates with that of others. Tables 5 and 6 give percentile rankings for the various scores made on Columbia and Junior Columbia Rounds, and Flint Rounds by college men and women. If an archer's score falls in the ninetieth percentile, it means that he is better than 90 per cent of the beginning college archers. Likewise, if the score is at the tenth percentile, it means the archer is better than only 10 per cent of his peers.

PROFILE RECORD

Plot scores here to check progress being made in the Columbia Round or Junior Columbia Round.

Profile Record of Scores										
Score										
510 +										
490–509										
470–489										
450–469										
430–449										
410–429										
390–409										
370–389										
350–369										
330–349										
310–329										
290–309										
270–289										
250–269										
230–249										
210–229										
190–209										
170–189										
150–169										
130–149										
110–129										
90–109										
70–89										
50–69										
30–49										
10–29										
Round	1	2	3	4	5	6	7	8	9	10

Plot scores made on Flint Rounds to show progress being made.

			Profile Record of Flint Round Scores						

Score									
175–184									
165–174									
155–164									
145–154									
135–144									
125–134									
115–124									
105–114									
95–104									
85– 94									
75– 84									
65– 74									
55– 64									
45– 54									
35– 44									
25– 34									
15– 24									
0– 14									
Round	1	2	3	4	5	6	7	8	9	10

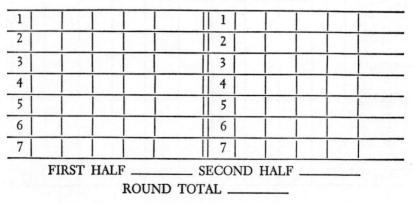

FIELD ARCHERY SCORE CARD—Flint Round

FIRST HALF _____ SECOND HALF _____

ROUND TOTAL _____

ARCHERY SCORE CARD—Columbia Round

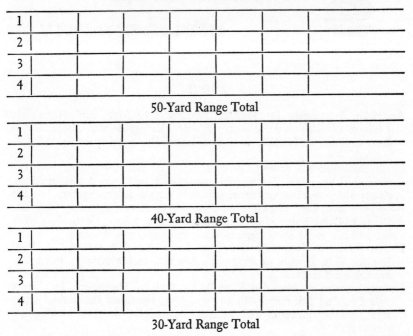

1						
2						
3						
4						

50-Yard Range Total

1						
2						
3						
4						

40-Yard Range Total

1						
2						
3						
4						

30-Yard Range Total

ROUND TOTAL ⎯⎯⎯⎯⎯⎯⎯⎯⎯⎯⎯⎯⎯⎯⎯⎯

BIBLIOGRAPHY

BOOKS

American Association for Health, Physical Education, and Recreation, Division of Girls and Women's Sports. *Archery-Riding Guide*. Washington, D.C.: AAHPER. Published biennially. Fundamentals and rules treated.

Burke, Edmund H. *Archery*. New York: Arco Publishing Co., Inc., rev. 1965. 143 pp., illus. Techniques, equipment, and rules for competition. Faults and corrective measures; primarily for the beginning target archer.

————. Archery (handbook). New York: Arco Publishing Co., Inc., 1954. 144 pp., illus. The do-it-yourself series. Many illustrations show the techniques of shooting, making equipment, and hunting.

Elmer, Robert P. *Target Archery*. New York: Alfred A. Knopf Co., 1946. 154 pp., illus. History of archery in America, tackle making, and fundamentals are discussed.

Forbes, Thomas A. *New Guide to Better Archery*. Harrisburg, Pa.: Stackpole Co., 2nd Ed. rev. 1960. 343 pp., illus. Furnishes the desired know-how for every phase of archery from learning to shoot to hunting the elusive deer.

Gannon, Robert. *The Complete Book of Archery*. New York: Coward-McCann, Inc., 1964. 256 pp., illus. Equipment, form, competition, how to avoid common shooting problems.

Haugen, Arnold O. and Harlan G. Metcalf. *Field Archery and Bowhunting*. New York: Ronald Press, 1963. 213 pp., illus. How to improve technique on the range and in the field.

Hickman, C. N., F. Nagler, and Paul E. Kopsteg. *Archery: The Technical Side*. Redlands, California: Box 388 NFAA, 1947. 281 pp., illus. A detailed analysis of the physics of bows and arrows, compilation of scientific and technical articles.

Hill, Howard, *Hunting the Hard Way*. Chicago: Follett Publishing Co., 1953. 318 pp., illus. Fascinating accounts of game hunting of all kinds.

————. *Wild Adventure*. Harrisburg, Pa.: Stackpole Co., 1954. 228 pp., illus. An absorbing collection of the true jungle thrills by an outstanding bow hunter.

Hochman, Louis. *The Complete Archery Book*. Greenwich, Conn.: Fawcett Publications, 1957. 144 pp., illus. The many illustrations help in explaining tackle making and the uses of archery.

Hodgkin, Adrian Eliot. *The Archer's Craft*. London: Faber & Faber, 1951. 222 pp., illus. Explains making tackle, shooting, and hunting with bows.

Hougham, Paul C. *The Encyclopedia of Archery*. New York: A. S. Barnes & Co., 1957. 202 pp., illus.

Hunt, W. Ben, and John J. Metz. *The Flat Bow*. New York: Bruce Publishing Co., 1948. Good instructions for the amateur who wishes to make his own tackle.

Keaggy, David J., Sr. *Power Archery*. Riderwood, Md.: Archery World Magazine, 1964.

Lambert, A. W. *Modern Archery*. New York: A. S. Barnes & Co., 1929. 306 pp., illus. A textbook on the art of shooting.

Love, Albert J. *Field Archery Technique*. Corpus Christi, Texas: Dotson Printing Co., 1956. 121 pp., illus. A comprehensive text that covers the subject of field archery.

National Archery Association. *Official Rules Book*. 2833 Lincoln Hgwy. E, Ronks, Pa. 17572. Covers rules for every type of round and information on setting up ranges.

National Field Archery Association. *Official Handbook of Field Archery*. Box H, Palm Springs, California 92262. A yearly publication covering rules, champions, and tournaments in field archery. Game statistics, shooting and hunting techniques also included.

National Rifle Association of America. *NRA Hunter Safety Handbook— Bow Hunting Supplement*. Washington, D.C.: NRA, 1957.

Perry, Walter. *Bucks and Bows*. Harrisburg, Pa.: Stackpole Co., 1954. 223 pp., illus. A good discussion of archery tackle, shooting techniques, and hunting deer.

Pope, Saxton. *Hunting with Bow and Arrow* (new ed.). New York: G. P. Putnam's Sons, 1947. 257 pp., illus. A classic on shooting and bow hunting. Dr. Pope learned archery from a full-blooded Indian named *Ishi*.

Reichart, Natalie, and Gilman Keasey. *Archery*. New York: Ronald Press, 3rd ed. rev., 1961. 78 pp. illus. The relaxed method of shooting is carefully outlined along with equipment, teaching methods, and types of competition. This book is better designed for teachers than for students.

Stalker, Tracy L. *How to Make Modern Archery Tackle*. Casein Company of America, 350 Madison Avenue, New York 17, N.Y.: 1948. 34 pp. Excellent instruction on how-to-do-it, for the home craftsman who desires to make his own tackle.

Whiffen, Larry C. *Shooting the Bow*. Milwaukee: The Bruce Publishing Co., 1946. 83 pp., illus. Describes the techniques of shooting.

FILMS

Available from Grayling Film Service, RR1, Grayling, Michigan 49738. All 16 mm., sound and color, mostly hunting movies. Free list available.

Available from Albin Films, 85544 Sunset Blvd., Hollywood 46, California: 16 mm. movies of Howard Hill, Joe Fries, Ande Vail, Russ Hoogerhyde, and Jim Lynch. Free list available.

Available from the Athletic Institute, 209 S. State Street, Chicago 4, Illinois: *Archery Filmstrip*, 35 mm., on history, shooting, aiming, and rules.

Available from Ben Pearson Company, Pine Bluff, Arkansas: Instructional and hunting films.

PERIODICALS

Archery—A Sportsman's Magazine Devoted to Hunting and Field. Official Publication of the National Field Archery Association, P.O. Box H, Palm Springs, California 92262.

Bow and Arrow. Published bimonthly by Gallant Publishing Co., 550 S. Citrus Ave., Covina, California 91722. Covers equipment, techniques, and hunting.

Tam and Archery World. Published monthly by Archer's Magazine Company, 24 South Reading Ave., Boyertown, Pennsylvania 19512. For bow hunters, field shooters, target shooters, and all sportsmen.

ORGANIZATIONS

American Archery Council, 100 East Ohio St., Chicago, Illinois 60611. Promulgating archery as recreation for fun and health. Part of its function is to promote archery in schools, colleges, and universities.

American Association for Health, Physical Education, and Recreation, Outdoor Education Project, 1201 Sixteenth St. N.W., Washington, D.C. 20036. Leadership preparation in archery through instructors' workshops. Director of Outdoor Education Project, Julian W. Smith, College of Education, Michigan State University, E. Lansing, Michigan.

Teela-Wooket Archery Camp, Roxbury, Vermont. Information director, Mrs. Edward B. Miller, 67 Old Stone Church Road, Upper Saddle River, New Jersey 07458. For the promotion of archery and instructor training.

National Archery Association of the United States, 2833 Lincoln Hgwy. E, Ronks, Pa. 17572. For layout of ranges; rules covering tournaments, championship rounds, clout, team, wand, cross-bow and flight shooting; sponsorship of tournaments.

National Collegiate Archery Coaches Association (sanctioned by NAA). Secretary-Treasurer, Mary E. Norckauer, Louisiana State University, Baton Rouge, Louisiana 70803. Promoting instruction and competition at the college and university level.

National Field Archery Association, Executive Offices: Box 967, Palm Desert, California 92260. For course construction, club formation, interpretation of rules concerning field archery, sponsorship of tournaments.